Tonight The Sky Cries With Me

COPYRIGHT

A Homegrown Book

First published in Great Britain, North America and the world in 2019 by Manhattan House.

This book first published 2019 by Manhattan House.
Copyright ©Jon Johanson 2019
Lyrics Copyright ©Blueberry Creek Publishing
(ASCAP) 2019

The right of Jon Johanson to be identified as the author of this work has been asserted in accordance with the Copyright, Designs and Patents Act 1988.

All characters and events in this publication are fictitious and any resemblance to real persons, living or dead, is purely coincidental.

All rights reserved, no part of this publication may by reproduced, stored in a retrieval system or transmitted in any form or by any means without the prior permission in writing of the publisher, not be otherwise circulated in any form of binding or cover other than that in which it is published with a similar condition, including this condition, being imposed on the subsequent purchaser.

A CIP catalogue record for this book is available from the British Library.

Homegrown Books
United States of America

Also available by Jon Johanson

Trailer Park Tales
Not My First Rodeo
Postcards From the Road
Scenes From A Dream
Winter, Spring, Summer, Fall
Songwriter
Waiting in the Wings
Prisoners of Love
Weekend Break
Trick
The Colour Of Love
Tall Stories and Short Scripts
The Lodge
Jack in the Box

www.jonjohanson.com

Contents

Broadway Cowboys
Gun
Mirror
Everybody's a star on Instagram
Dancing on the Grave of Jim Crow
Whatever Happened to You?
Crowded Solitude
Portrait of a Storm
I Know I'm In Here Somewhere
A New Chapter
I Can't Remember My Name
Ballad of Joshua Tree
Ballad of the Last Coyote
Blueprint of a Love Affair
H
Averie Grace
Dark Cloud
Hiraeth
If I Could Go Back
Rebel Heart
Psycho Daisy Mae
Yesterday Today was Tomorrow
Do You Ever Think Of Me?
Protect

Contents (continued)

The Playgrounds of our Minds
Wave
Laurel Canyon
Front Porch Swing
Regrets
Lighthouse
Bridge of Fate
Healing Waters
When Does the End Starts?
Ended
A Safe Place to Land

Broadway Cowboys

Little man
in big cowboy boots
His cowgirl is running late
Touching up her roots
Wannabe cowboy
Stetson on his head
Cowgirl closes her eyes
Wishing Haggard was there instead

Line dancing
He leads her around the floor
She wants to dance right out of there
But can't find the door
She wears a short denim skirt
Showing off her legs
She'd change it all
If she were a teenager again

All the Broadway Cowboys
Honky tonk-ing
on a Saturday night
Not a horse in sight
Anyway they can't ride
They ride into town
In their SUV's
Trying to escape
The lives that they lead

He leans against the bar
JD in his hand
Listening to the music
Of the resident band

She sees a tall dark stranger
She knows the type too well
He smiles across the room
But he's smiling at someone else

It's late after midnight
Bars begin to close
They slowly make their way back
To the motel room
that's their home
At least for the weekend
At least for this dream
The music begins to fade
Into someone else's dream

Neon lights
Electric noise
Bucking bulls
And other toys
Plastic guns
Sad bought joys
But it's a way of life
For Broadway cowboys

Gun

Shot
Can't take that bullet back
Fire
A random attack
Senseless
It has no meaning
Cold
A man without feeling

Dead
Lying in a pool of blood
Slain
To prove someone is tough
Worthless
Is how a life is viewed
Gone
Nothing left to lose

Lost
Second lasts a lifetime
Hope
Crying for a lifeline

Mirror

Hey,
it's been a while
Guess we lost touch
Somewhere
along the way
You know how it is
Life gets in the way
And time
Just seems to fly by
So fast
A blink of the eye
And life has passed you by

But anyway
How are you
Are you good
How is life treating you?
Are you happy?
You deserve to be
But
you seem quiet
Withdrawn
And there's something
about your eyes that's changed
Something that is missing

They seem
I don't know
Cold
Empty
sad
Do you cry often?

You used to be so full of life
The life of every party
You were always ready
to take on the world
You were always so strong
So what happened
What changed
Do you smile
At all?

When was the last time
You laughed out loud
Where's that spark
That always got you through
Where's the fire
that used to burn
inside of you

I'm sorry
I best be going
it's been good though
To catch up
See how you are
We really mustn't leave it so long
Next time
I'll keep in touch
But I hate to leave you here
Alone
like this
Will you be okay?

You know where I am
If you ever need to talk
I'm always here
The mirror on your wall

Everybody's a star on Instagram

Don't look at the camera
Get the right pose
All the young women
Forget their clothes
All to be noticed
Justify their lives
Bloggers beware
When your life is a lie
Can't take it back
Once it's out there
It's out there
Forever
Delete that old lover
But does anyone care
Filtered or not
Your life in a frame
Zoom in zoom out
Get that angle again
In search of fame
You have no shame
You buy a thousand followers
Hoping others will follow you
What will it take
For you to see that none of it is true
So busy faking your life
There's no time left for you
Selfie queen will fade
How will you feel
When you've sacrificed your life
And none of it was real

Dancing on The Grave of Jim Crow

Ante-bellum
Civil War
Don't treat me
like a slave no more

Lied to rest
But still rears its head
Equal rights
but the ghost's not dead

Tell the truth
What you see
What's in a color
The blood we bleed

Prove he's dead
Dig up his grave
Although he hides
He's still alive today

Reconstruction
we're all the same
Pass the law
reversed again

Ain't no threat
Don't take my freedom away
Ignorance
Fears turns into hate

I'm just a singer
with a minstrel show
But I dance
Every night
on the grave
of Jim Crow

Whatever Happened to You

I often wonder what happened
To people I used to know
School friends
People who came into my life
For whatever reason
Some stayed for a short while
Others
A lifetime
At my age
I wonder if they're still alive
Maybe they've moved on
Maybe they've died
I know many have
I miss them
The memories though are still alive
Paris
Cardiff
Santa Barbara
LA
and more
They're all there
Ready and lined up for a rewind
A rerun
And as with all of us
We followed our separate paths
Had our own families
Made our new homes
I'm not one though
For looking back
too much
I hope there's still enough ahead
Of me
For me

To look forward to
But still I wonder
Where they might be
I've travelled across the world
Moved many miles away
And lost touch
Somewhere along the way
And mistakes I made
Don't seem to matter anymore
I've moved on
I learned
Life is short
And to take it all in
Make every day count
I guess the older you get
The days ahead are fewer
More precious
therefore
But I often wonder
Whatever happened to you?

Crowded Solitude

It's crowded
in this solitude
I often bully myself
Asking myself questions
that I know
I have no answers for
beating myself up
insisting the mirror
is lying to me

I feel smothered
when I don't reply to your texts
straight away
when I don't return your calls
straight away
You bombard me
with calls
and more texts
is it insecurity
whatever it is
It's pushing me away

I feel suffocated
It seems I'm not allowed to be me
There's someone else
you'd rather I'd be

Is it control
that you seek
you try to control me
You should know me better than that

I am drowning
slowly
in these stormy seas
of your life
your love
that should be a life line
is holding me down
pushing me further away
from you

Portrait of a Storm

In the shadows of vultures
That circle overhead
Waiting
for the moment
To kill the dead

A wolf howls
at my door
Then hides beneath the willow tree
Hold on
to the olive branch
And come and rescue me

And as lightning strikes
And thunder roars
The canvas destroyed
in the rain that stills falls
Leaving a portrait
A portrait of a storm

The sky gets darker
Seek shelter to be safe
I have to try and ignore
The sirens
calling my name

Tornado warning
Electricity in the air
The wind grows stronger
Carries away words
left unsaid

Don't cower
And stay and hide inside
Waiting for the storm to pass
You'll die inside
Don't waste your life

The dark clouds finally pass
There's an eerie silence left
But for the wings of the vultures
that still circle
overhead

I Know I'm In Here Somewhere

I know I'm in here somewhere
I seem to have misplaced myself
Strangers who don't know me
Think I'm someone else

But they don't know me
The me I really am
Sometimes if feels I don't know me either
Just part of someone else's plan

But if you look closely
Look into my eyes
You might still see me somewhere
in there
and hear a desperate cry

It seems I lost myself
In the shadows of life's games
I allowed myself to disappear
and hide behind this face

There has to be a balance
Who I used to be
Who I am today
I am not in control though
It seems I have no say

Many factors mitigate
Many people have their say
It feels like I'm outnumbered
I'm put into my place

I know I'm in here somewhere
But could someone help me please
I need to find myself again
I need to be released

A New Chapter

Life is a journey
Life is a book
Life of chances that I took

Life is a story
That unfolds
Whisper secrets never told

It's time for me to write
a new chapter in my life
and this time
I might get it right

Gonna write
a new chapter in my life

Life is a play
follow the plot
Thankful for what I've got

The final act
The final page
Reveals mistakes that I made

It's time for me to write
a new chapter in my life
and this time
I might get it right
Gonna write
a new chapter in my life

The characters in my life
Write the stories I never tell
Pages turned
Pages burnt

Will you be in my story?
Will you be my story?

I Can't Remember My Name

You know you've torn out
the very heart of me
You've taken away who I am
I'm in your shadow
When my light
once shined so bright
I haven't the strength
left to fight
You're playing games
with my mind

You slowly stripped away
any pride I had
You've stolen all the dreams
I ever had
You've chipped away,
day after day
Until I'm scared to say
The words I want to say
All the things I've done
Slowly fade

I can't remember my name
I can't remember my name
You've put out the fire
You've put out the flame
You've taken all the drive in me away
And I can't remember my name

You use my love
for you
against me

You turn around
everything I say
You twist my words
Like a knife
inside my heart
Is it part
of a master plan?
That I forget
who I really am

You discard me
when I try to tell you
how I feel
You dismiss me
You put me down
Criticize me all the time
Your words cut me
more than any knife
You make me feel so small
So worthless

I'm a shadow
of who I used to be
When I'm alone
I don't recognize me
Is this control
your insecurity
More than ever
You don't really know me
Have you ever really known me?
Do I even know myself
Anymore?

The Ballad of Joshua Tree

Bird flies
Desert high
An angel looking back

Night sky
Sister cries
Laying down the tracks

Preach
Joshua Tree
Show the way
To New Orleans
Shooting star
A spirit lost
Nineteen seventy-three

Motel
No tell
Check in number eight
Last fix
Twenty-six
Always checks out late

Don't be sad
Don't go back
Can't you see
Horses wild and free

Hear the song
wind so strong
Hickory
Ballad of Joshua Tre

The Ballad of the Last Coyote

Life hurts
Pain is real
It scars
It heals
We move on
And do it all again
We cry like fools
Under the coyote moon

Lost chance
Hope fades
Sun sets
Convict prays
Secrets new
We hide away
Shelter from the truth
Under the coyote moon

As the last coyote howls
Singing his own sad song
A ballad of light and dark
The coyote moves along

Blueprint of a Love Affair

I could get down
on my knees
And beg
for your forgiveness
And I will
If that's what you want me to do
Need me to do
I can promise you
That it will never happen again
But I know I've hurt you
I need you to know
I never meant to

I could say
it didn't mean anything
I'm not sure that would help
I've betrayed you
I've betrayed what we had
All the memories we made
Erased
Could we try again
Could we get it back again?
It would never be the same
Perhaps that would be good
Perhaps it could be better
Not just the same

H

You revel in your own words
An audience who never heard
Delusional thinking
hurt
When they tried to steal your work
You live on the glory
of little success
God is confused when you confess
Which God are you praying to today
Your faith will forever change
You don't listen to other people's views
But then again no one listens to you
When you try to attain
that stature that you seek
Forgotten albums
long ago released
Although they never really sold
they opened doors
which soon closed
Now you preach
to an invisible congregation
While you deny the existence
of a true nation
You sit in your house
all by yourself
Trying your best
to be somebody else
Someone you're not
but would like to be
Perhaps you'll wake up
and it's all been just a dream

Averie Grace

You don't know me
Not at all
Perhaps you never will
But my blood
Runs through you
Always will

No one told me
About you
I found out
Just by chance
I saw your picture
Someone had posted
The tears I cried
Were for myself
Looking at you
So beautiful

What can I do
To make it up to you
What can I say
That could start to explain

How can I make you understand
When I don't understand it
Myself

There's no one else
That's to blame
It's only me
Who's lost
And now I know the cost
Guess it's too late
To make amends
That's why I feel so sad
You can't change the past

I wipe away the tears
As I look at your face
I'd give anything to hold you
Averie Grace

Dark Cloud

There's a dark cloud
Above me
I've seen it there before
I try to stay strong
Ride out the storm
It's always darkest
Just before dawn

There's a tunnel
That I'm lost in
And I'm carrying
a heavy weight
I struggle to walk
Make my way
To the light
of a new day

Just let me be
I'll find my way out
From under this dark cloud
I'll cry my tears
Work it all out
And escape from this dark cloud

I know
you want to help me
but I need to do this
myself
I've got to get through it
myself
so I come out
the other end

Hiraeth

Land of my fathers
Land where I was born
Land where my father died
Even now, I still mourn

The ghosts in the valleys
Still work deserted mines
The children of their children
Cry for a different time

I climb the highest mountain
A snow hill that touches the sky
I head south for the beacon
Guided by city lights

I grew up on city streets
In a time long since past
A dream like childhood
I knew could never last

I am dreaming
It's okay
I am dreaming
It's a play
Look under my dreams
Walk to the isle by the sea

Cariad fills my heart
Tears fill my eyes
I can't go gently
I rage into the night

I leave footprints
in white sand
The rugged coast
protects the wild
Dunes that hide the answers
To questions
of a curious child

If I Could Go Back

If I could go back
Would I change anything
Would I do it all again
keep it all the same

I wish I could go back
Live it all again
But you can't go back
the one chance you've got to take

So make each day count
Time wasted you can't get back
Don't regret in later years
The time you can't get back

I wish I could go back
Live my life all over again
Go through it all again
Laughter and the pain

I can look back
I prefer to look forward
I have my memories
But so many more
to make

Rebel Heart

There's a little devil
in her big angel heart
She plays by the rules
But she's a rebel at heart
She'd hang the rapist
cries for the victim
Buts she's promised herself
She won't cry for herself

She hates the racists
But would fight
for their freedom of speech
She dresses up
But prefers to dress down

She holds her patience
But never suffers fools
She plays to win
But she never minds to lose

She knows who she is
And who she'd like to be
She always listens
But is never scared
to disagree

She picks her battles wisely
Hates to be at war
When words
are the only weapons used

Psycho Daisy Mae

She tells me
all her secrets
She tells me
all her lies
She tells me
that she loves me
A love she will then deny
She'll smile at me
At you
And then stab us in the back
Don't believe
All that you see
Her façade soon starts to crack

I watch her eyes
I watch them stray
I don't trust a single word
she says
She won't leave me alone
For days
Is she crazy
Or simply insane
Psycho Daisy Mae

She changes her moods
With a blink of an eye
I never know where I stand
Or with whom she lies
There's no smoking gun
But she fires bullets at me
She looks lovingly at me
As she watches me bleed
She tries to control me
Pulling on my heartstrings
A puppet master
But I can cut the strings
Anytime I choose
Anytime she lets me
But I've got too much to lose

Yesterday Today was Tomorrow

Time
can hide
away
the pain
But some scars
never truly heal
They'll always remain
Cry
tears of joy
Cry
tears of sorrow
Yesterday
Today
was tomorrow
and tomorrow
today
will be yesterday

Do You Ever Think of Me?

It's been a long time
Since we said goodbye
Since I last saw you
When you had tears in your eyes
I hear you've moved on
Found somebody new
I hope you're happy
Hope they're good to you

When it's late at night
When you just can't get to sleep
Are you scared to dream?
Do you ever dream of me?

We were young
So long ago
We grew up
We grew apart
We let each other go
Two broken hearts
No one was to blame
After all we'd been through
It was just a shame
And still I think of you

There should be no regrets
We can't change the past
But at the time
We both thought
our love would last

But I often think of us
And how it used to be
I often think of you
Do you ever think of me?

Protect

I can try
to protect you
From the world
But I can't
protect you
From yourself

You can protect me
from the world
But you can't protect me
From myself

She told me
she'd protect me
from the world
I wish she could protect me
from myself

The Playgrounds of Our Minds

There's something sad
About an empty playground
An empty swing
That still moves
gently
In the wind
The ghosts of innocence
Whisper
Taunt you
Haunt you
As they laugh
In the wind
As memories
Ride
The carousel horses
Showing no remorse
Endlessly
They ride
On the roundabout
That is life
We try to go
Faster
And never want it to end
When we are young
It seems like the roundabout
Is never going to stop
But when it does go faster
We try to get off
We try to jump
But scared
we'll get hurt
We stay on

It's a cruel world

Walking through your old schoolyard
Deserted
In the rain
Echoes of laughter
And tears
Shelter you
Follow you
Through the years
Through the school

Empty corridors
Full of ghosts
A bell rings
Once again
But only in your head

As we get older
We remember friends
We lost touch with
Friends
We simply lost touch with
We thought
we were immortal
It's a shock
now
To find friends
Have dead
When they remain
so clearly
alive
In our heads

Wave

I wave to Jesus
He's standing
by the side of the road
I offer Him
a ride
He carries
such a heavy load

He smiles
to me
Gently
bows His head
His arms
open wide
Safety's
always there

But I drive on
Out of my comfort zone
But I can't get lost
when
I don't know
where I'm going
which direction
where I'm heading to
I can't be lost though
when
I know my way
home

Laurel Canyon

There's a magic in the air every night
Lights from the City of Angels shine so bright
Ladies of the canyon's last refrain
Stardust in our hair
still remains

The harmonies linger on in my head
Someone says its Déjà Vu all over again
Mama waves at me as I pass her by
Hypnotized
by her smile

Laurel Canyon
Calling my nameLaurel Canyon
Calling me back home
Laurel Canyon

The Salford kid hangs outside the country store
Stephen still doesn't Tork anymore
The young grow younger everyday
I just hope Crosby now
remembers his name

The spirits of the canyon remain
A coyote cries over the dead
They still live there
In the hills
As the vultures from the press
circle overhead

Doors open on Wonderland
Jimi's in a purple haze
Janis just gave another piece of her heart
Frank has got his mothers to play

I hear the canyon calling my name
I know it is time I went home again
Back to Laurel Canyon

Front Porch Swing

See the swing
On the front porch
Of our old house
I'd sit there every night
When I was a kid
Planning out my life

I'd sit
and watch life go by
Not much happened
in my home town

I learned to play guitar
On that front porch
I cried when
My heart first got broken
On that front porch

And I'd sit on that porch
with friends
We'd talk for hours
about nothing
Everything
Friends I'm sad to say
I long ago lost touch with
I moved away

Everything changed
From my childhood days
When this boy became a man
I go back
Some nights in my dreams
And see
The swing is still there
Along with so many memories
The porch is just the same
As it was all those years ago
It helped this boy to grow
Our front porch swing

Regrets

Will I live
to not regret it
A moment of madness
Spontaneity
Or insanity
Feeling reckless
As I drive into my life

If you've lived a life
of regrets
Rather than the things
that you did do
Are they regrets
for what you didn't do?
Not regrets at what you said
But for the things
you didn't say

Do you ever think about dying?
How you'll pass
I don't mean to be morbid
But it's something
we never talk about
But you must think about it
To yourself
Sometimes

Will I love
And regret it
Regret you
But you can't regret love
I might live
To regret
Mistakes that I've made
But I could never
Regret you

Lighthouse

In this sea of life
there are many ships
that pass in the night
Briefly
lovers
For the night
For a short while

But you
You shine
Like a beacon
A lighthouse
Whose light
guides me
And lights the way
You save me
From drowning
or being shipwrecked
lost at sea
lost on the rocks

You are my lifeboat
You are my lighthouse

Bridge of Fate

Danny's got a gun
in his hand
Wants to be king
for a day,
a hero
forgotten
a trail
of betrayal
lives destroyed

Lost sight
Of the truth
Danny got lost
Somewhere
between his dreams
And his nightmares
Lost his grip
On reality

Reaching for his castle
In the sky
As the rain
Washes away
not only pain
But blood
Of souls lost

For him
There is no escape
The traitors have to die
He waits to pay the toll
With his soul
To cross
the Bridge of Fate
That can take him back
Across the wind
That sealed his fate

Healing Waters

Healing waters
Lord
Let them rain
down
on me
Let them
heal me

Raging waters
Lord
Help me
to sail through
Help me
To get through

When Does The End Start?

When will it end
Where to start
Trying to make sense
Of something
so senseless

Trying to reason
When there's
no reason at all
When it all seems crazy
There's no sanity
To rationalize

What's the point?
When it all seems pointless
Where does it end
Where to start
When does the end start?

Ended

We ended up
on the beach
3 am in the morning
It was deserted
The lights of the angels
Lit up the beach
The Ferris wheel
The sound of the ocean
Caressing the sand

You dared me
to go swimming
And laughed
when I said
I had nothing to wear
You undressed
And ran into the cold sea
Naked
And beckoned me
to join you
Which I did
How could I refuse you?
The water was cold
But you warmed me
We lay on the beach
And made love
And fall asleep
Until the sunrise
woke us
We ended up
in a motel
On Santa Monica boulevard

A Safe Place To Land

I know you're scared
To fall

But I'll catch you
Like
you've never been caught
before

Just reach out
And take my hand
We'll find a safe place
To land

Printed in Poland
by Amazon Fulfillment
Poland Sp. z o.o., Wrocław